ALL YOU NEED IS A PENCIL

THE STUCK IN A CAR, PLANE, OR TRAIN ACTIVITY BOOK

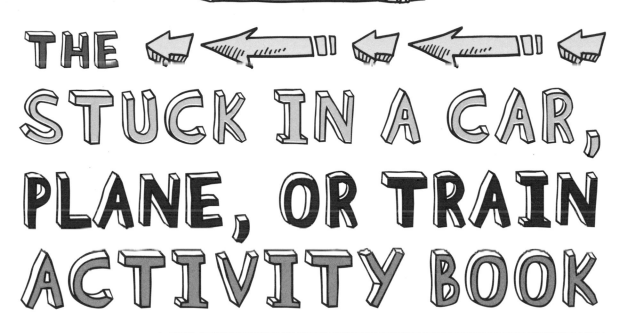

Games, Doodling, Puzzles, and More!

JOE RHATIGAN

ILLUSTRATIONS BY ANTHONY OWSLEY

imagine!

An Imagine Book
Published by Charlesbridge
85 Main Street, Watertown, MA 02472
(617) 926-0329
www.charlesbridge.com

Text copyright © 2014 by Joseph Rhatigan
Interior and cover design by Melissa Gerber
Illustrations copyright © 2014 by Charlesbridge Publishing, Inc.
Printed in China, December 2014.

ISBN 978-1-62354-008-1
4 6 8 10 9 7 5

For information about custom editions, special sales, premium and corporate purchases, please contact Charlesbridge Publishing at specialsales@charlesbridge.com

YOUR VACATION BEGINS . . . NOW!

The people who say "life is a journey" and "getting there is half the fun" aren't the ones sitting in the backseat of a hot minivan for twelve hours while their parents argue over whether to listen to the GPS or follow the map to the next Best Western. Yes, traveling can be fun; however, the hours of sitting around waiting to get there can be agonizing. Well, with this book, your vacation begins *before* you even get wherever it is you're going.

Whether riding in a car, airplane, boat, train, or hovercraft (or waiting to ride in one of these), you'll find something interesting to do right here. Every page is bursting with all sorts of activities, quizzes, puzzles, games, and doodles to take your mind off the fact that you're *not* there yet. Plus, there's nothing to plug in, no batteries required, and Wi-Fi hotspots aren't necessary. All you need is something to write with, and your sweaty car, airplane, boat, train, or hovercraft ride will be the fun journey everyone tells you it's supposed to be.

Send me a postcard when you get there!

WACKY WORDS OF WEIRDNESS

Fill in the blanks with the words from the list that sound like the words that best complete the sentences. The trick here is that each syllable of the words in the list acts as a full word itself in the answer. For example: He's very sick, but he won't <u>digest</u> yet. *Digest* sounds like ***die just***: He's very sick, but he won't <u>die just</u> yet. **Answers on page 137.**

WORDS

commonplace

detest

doozy

easy

loner

realize

research

stuffy

tenor

tire

1. When you're done, _____ your test on my desk.

2. I had to _____ ten dollars because she was a little short.

3. _____ coming with us or not?

4. Whenever our dog runs away, _____ for her.

5. I'll need _____ eleven carrots for the recipe.

6. _____ have enough money to buy us ice cream?

7. The _____ knows could fill an encyclopedia!

8. That teddy bear looks like it has _____.

9. If the dog wanders off, you'll have to _____ up.

10. I forgot to study and failed _____.

TRAVEL QUOTES

Sitting in the car, train, boat, or plane with your family? If you hear any of them say one of the quotes below, put their name in the blank.

"I have to go to the bathroom," said _____.

"I think we're lost," said _____.

"Are we there yet?" asked _____.

"I'm hungry," said

_____.

"Leave me alone," said

_____.

"My stomach hurts," said

_____.

"I'm hot," said

_____.

"I'm cold," said _____.

"I'm bored," said _____.

"Where can I plug in my iPod?" asked _____.

"How come nobody listens to me?" said _____.

"Put your feet down," said _____.

"Stop touching me!" screamed _____.

"I don't like this movie," exclaimed _____.

"Something smells really bad in here," said _____.

"Don't make me turn this car around," said _____.

"I think I forgot my _____," said _____.

"I need the _____ in my luggage," said _____.

"Where should I put my gum?" asked _____.

"Ewww, who took off his shoes?" asked _____.

"I wanna go home," said _____.

"Are we going too fast?" asked _____.

"Don't you think you should use a map?" asked _____.

Design your train cars on the tracks.

GOMOKU

This is a traditional board game that's easy to play with paper and pencil.

The Object

Be the first player to get a row of five either horizontally, vertically, or diagonally.

What You Need

2 players
Pencil

What You Do

1. Decide who will be X and who will be O.
2. X goes first and places her mark on the game board.
3. Then it's O's turn to place his mark on the board.
4. Keep taking turns until someone has five in a row.

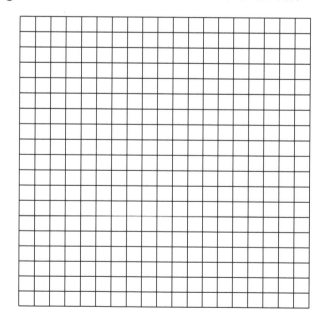

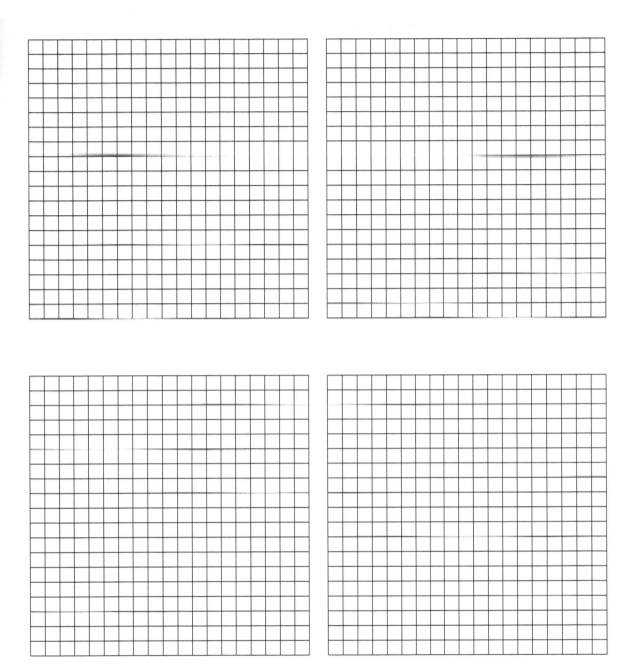

WORD JUMBLES

Unscramble the words in each puzzle, and then use the shaded letters to form a word that fits in the sentence. Use the empty space on the pages to figure out the words. One trick is to place all the letters of a scrambled word in a circle. For example, the letters YPHPA may be difficult to sort out, but when placed like this:

P
P   H
A Y

it's easier to see the word is **happy**.
Answers on page 137.

1. How much does a pirate pay for corn? A _____

YTCI

FNUONICT

EELBR

EPRGA

2. What do you call a guy with a really flexible toe? _____
(All clues are people with one name.)

APEONLON

YEBCOEN

RECH

CRNIPE

TSGIN

12

3. What did the buffalo say to her departing child? _____, _____ (two words)

YATDO

☐ ▢ ☐ ☐ ▢

BCTESI

▢ ☐ ☐ ▢ ☐ ☐

XAFNPD

☐ ☐ ☐ ☐ ▢

TSGDIE

☐ ☐ ☐ ☐ ▢

4. What do cats eat for breakfast? _____ _____ (two words)

DEEOR

▢ ▢ ☐ ☐ ▢

CICKL

▢ ☐ ▢ ☐ ☐

EMITAPN

☐ ☐ ▢ ☐ ▢ ▢ ☐

TRIESS

▢ ▢ ☐ ▢ ☐ ☐

5. What do you call a bear with no teeth? A _____ _____ (two words)

IONRCAMA

▢ ☐ ☐ ☐ ☐ ☐ ☐ ☐

SCEMLU

▢ ☐ ☐ ☐ ☐ ▢

REETRG

▢ ☐ ▢ ☐ ☐ ☐

VBRRYEA

▢ ☐ ☐ ☐ ☐ ☐ ▢

CAN YOU RAED TIHS?

Some people say that it doesn't matter what order most of the letters in words are in when you're reading, and that the only important thing is that the first and last letters are where they should be. Try to read the sentences below and see what you think! **Answers on page 137.**

Can you read these nursery rhymes?

1. Mray had a llttie lmab
Woshe fceele was wihte as sonw;
And eevyrhwree taht Mray wnet,
The lmab was srue to go.

2. Old Knig Cloe was a mrery old suol
And a mrery old suol was he;
He cllaed for his ppie and he cllaed for his bwol
And he cllaed for his fdiderls trehe.

3. Llitte boy bule, cmoe bolw yuor hron.
The seehp's in the moeadw, the cow's in the cron.
But werhe's the boy who lokos aetfr the seehp?
He's uednr a hcatsyak, fsat aelesp.

TIHS IS GVINIG ME A HADECHAE!

Now try these familiar sayings:

4. Enithvyerg hneppas for a raeosn.

5. Aylwas a besdiriamd, nveer the birde.

6. His brak is wrose tahn his btie.

7. A pneny seavd is a pneny eearnd.

8. Dno't trohw the bbay out wtih the bhtawtaer.

9. Solw and setday wnis the rcae.

Finally, try reading these famous quotes:

10. Wlel dnoe is beettr tahn wlel siad.

11. Atttduie is a lttile tnihg taht mkeas a big dffiecnere.

12. Tnikinhg is the hraesdt wrok tehre is, wcihh is plbaroby why so few egagne in it.

13. Mndis are lkie paarechtus: Tehy olny fiotuncn wehn tehy are oepn.

14. Eeryvnihtg soulhd be mdae as smpile as piblosse . . . but not smpleir.

15. Tentwy yreas form now you wlil be mroe dppisaoetnid by the tinghs you ddin't do tahn by the oens you did.

PLAN YOUR ULTIMATE VACATION

You have one week to spend anywhere in the world.
Where would you go? What would you do?

Location: _____

Who's coming with you: _____

What you will bring with you: _____

Plan Your Week

Day 1:

_____
_____
_____

Day 2:

_____
_____
_____

Day 3:

_____
_____
_____

Day 4:

_____

_____

Day 5:

_____

_____

Day 6:

_____

_____

Day 7:

_____

_____

FINISH THESE CREEPY CRITTERS

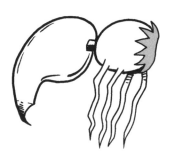

TONGUE TRIPS

Try saying these foreign tongue twisters out loud! Once you get the hang of it, suck on an ice cube until your mouth feels numb. Spit out what's left of the cube and recite them again. Or eat a bunch of crackers and recite while they're still in your mouth. (Don't try this in the back of the car!)

Del pelo al codo y del codo al pelo, del codo al pelo y del pelo al codo.

Language: Spanish
Translation: From the hair to the elbow and from the elbow to the hair, from the elbow to the hair and from the hair to the elbow.

Kale kakuku kadogo ka kaka kako wapi kaka?

Language: Swahili
Translation: Where are your chickens, brother?

Ke oke okoo, mo ko ko ke ya shi ko ko ko.

Language: Ga, the native language of Ghana
Translation: If you refuse to take it, someone else will, and will go knocking knocking knocking on the door with it.

Niwa no niwa ni wa, niwa no niwatori wa niwaka ni wani o tabeta.

Language: Japanese
Translation: In Mr. Niwa's garden, two chickens suddenly ate a crocodile.

Ganan gidel dagan bagan dagan gadol gadal bagan.

Language: Hebrew
Translation: A gardener grew grain in the garden, big grain grew in the garden.

Hele wawai o ka malamalama, ka malamalama, o ka malamalama, hele wawai o ka malamalama, ka malamalama o ke Akua.

Language: Hawaiian
Translation: I am walking in the light, in the light, in the light, I am walking in the light, in the light of God.

Luuqa mlaqqam il-laaqi laaq-laaqa il-qara li qala u-qela bil-aaqal.

Language: Maltese
Translation: Luke nicknamed the toady, licked the gourd, which he picked and fried carefully.

Kärpänen sanoi kärpäselle, tuu kattoon kattoon kun kaveri tapettiin tapettiin!

Language: Finnish
Translation: Says a fly to a fly, look there on the ceiling, your buddy is sticking on the ceiling and is dead.

Knut satt vid en knut och knöt en knut. När Knut knutit knuten var knuten knuten.

Language: Swedish
Translation: Knut was sitting in a corner and tying a knot. When Knut had tied the knot, the knot was tied.

Láttam szőrös hörcsögöt. Éppen szörpöt szörcsögött. Ha a hörcsög szörpöt szörcsög rátörnek a hörcsög görcsök.

Language: Hungarian
Translation: I saw a bearded hamster. It was lapping syrup. If a hamster is lapping syrup, it will be seized with a hamster-clamp.

Je suis ce que je suis, et si je suis ce que je suis, qu'est-ce que je suis?

Language: French
Translation: I am what I am, and if I am what I am, what am I?

Naygah gerleen geeleen gerleemern jahl gerleen geeleen gerleemeego naegah gerleen geeleen gerleemern moht saengeen geeleen gerleemeeda.

Language: Korean
Translation: I draw a giraffe picture, a pretty giraffe picture. You draw a giraffe picture, an ugly giraffe picture.

Trentatré Trentini entrarono a Trento, tutti e trentatré, trotterellando.

Language: Italian
Translation: Thirty-three Trentonians came to Trento, all thirty-three trotting.

Vissende vissers die vissen naar vissen, maar vissende vissers die vangen vaak bot. De vis waar de vissende vissers naar vissen vindt vissende vissers vervelend en rot.

Language: Dutch
Translation: Fishermen who go fishing for fish and fishermen who fish often catch flounders. The fish that the fishing fishermen fish for find fishermen that go fishing annoying and beastly.

UShabalala washabalala neshumi losheleni emshinini kashukela eshashalazini laseShowe.

Language: Zulu
Translation: Mr. Shabalala disappeared with one rand at the sugar factory in the valley of Eshowe.

OFF WITH ITS HEAD!

Cut off the first letter of what's being "beheaded" in each of the following questions to see what's left behind. For example: Behead eye water and leave behind a body part. Eye water = tear; beheaded tear = ear. **Answers on page 138.**

1. Behead a baby's bed and leave a bone.
2. Behead a monster and leave a direction.
3. Behead a national park worker and leave rage.
4. Behead a car accident and leave an allergic reaction.
5. Behead an allergic reaction and leave campfire remains.
6. Behead what you do with your fingers and leave an exclamation when something hurts.
7. Behead Blackbeard and leave angry.
8. Behead a tale and leave a British sympathizer during the Revolutionary War.
9. Behead soft fatty body tissue and leave a scientist's workplace.
10. Behead a rock that starts fires and leave fabric fuzz.
11. Behead what thinks and leave falling water.
12. Behead a hoax and leave a pork product.
13. Behead a type of reef and leave a type of test.
14. Behead where water comes out a pipe and leave a facial expression of unhappiness.
15. Behead a facial expression of unhappiness and get the opposite of *in*.

Now behead the first letter to get something that *sounds like* what remains, but is spelled differently. For example: Behead a small storage shelter (shed) and leave what's above your neck (hed = head).

16. Behead a public address and leave a yummy fruit.
17. Behead an action word and get a medicinal plant.
18. Behead a large water-bound mammal and get frozen rain.
19. Behead not the second or the fourth and leave a bunch of animals.
20. Behead breakfast pork strips and leave hurtin'.

Now come up with your own:

Behead _____ and leave _____.

Behead _____ and leave _____.

Behead _____ and leave _____.

Behead _____ and leave _____.

Behead _____ and leave _____.

Behead _____ and leave _____.

Behead _____ and leave _____.

Behead _____ and leave _____.

Behead _____ and leave _____.

Behead _____ and leave _____.

FAST FOOD

Don't eat it—draw it! You have five minutes to draw pictures of as many types of food as you can think of on these two pages. Time yourself.

JUST SITTING THERE GAMES

These are all games you can play when you're just sitting there in the backseat, plane seat, train seat, or boat deck waiting to get where you're going!

DON'T SAY *YES* OR *NO*

Players cannot answer *yes* or *no* to the questions asked of them. For example: Do you have brown eyes? Well, they're dark in color—lighter than black; the same color as my hair. Take turns asking questions.

PRETZEL LOGIC

Ask your travel mates, "Can you put your right hand in such a position that the left hand can't possibly touch it?" Let them tie themselves in knots before telling them the best way to do this is to grab your left elbow with your right hand.

CATEGORIES

Everyone agrees on a category of things (sports, celebrities, spices, etc.). Now take turns naming an item that belongs in the category. If you can't think of something, you're out. Keep going until there's only one player left. You can make things more challenging by picking names of things in alphabetical order. If the category is food, for example, and the first player names *apple*, the next player might pick *banana*, and the next player *coconut*.

WHATNOT

Have one player put her fingers in her ears while the others choose a verb that describes an activity, such as *eat*, *drive*, or *sleep*. Now it's up to her to discover the secret word by asking questions—but she has to substitute the word *whatnot* for the word: "Can I *whatnot* at school?"

or "Can a cat whatnot?" The other players must give (truthful!) yes or no answers.

THROW IT

The first player announces a three-letter word, and then quickly the next player has to come up with three words that start with the letters of the word, in order. For example, *cat* can inspire "can, apple, toaster." The other players must come up with three new words, not repeating any previously used ones ("car, ant, tooth"). Keep going until someone goofs or draws a blank.

DON'T SAY IT

One player decides on a letter that can no longer be spoken. He then asks each player a question (not a yes-or-no question) that must be answered without using the forbidden letter. Creative answers are encouraged, but not nonsense responses. For example, if the forbidden letter is *F* and the questioner asks, "What has gills and swims in the ocean?" the response could be, "A man in snorkel gear." As the questioner moves around the car, if a player takes longer than thirty seconds to respond or if he gives a crazy answer, he's out. The last remaining player becomes the questioner in the next round.

!

MAYBE WE SHOULD TRY ANOTHER GAME!

Can you identify each of these places by its outline? Oh, and by the way, not all of them are right-side up! **Answers on page 138.**

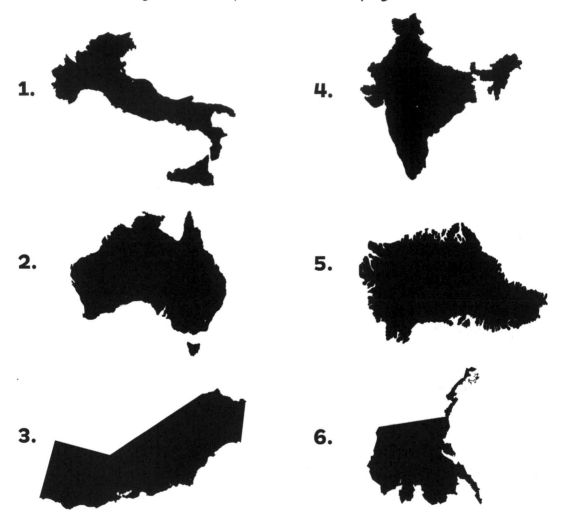

1.

2.

3.

4.

5.

6.

7.

8.

9.

10.

11.

12.

13.

14.

15.

DON'T THINK TWICE: THE BODIES OF WATER EDITION

Answer the questions below as quickly as possible without putting too much thought into them. Time yourself and see how many you get right. Don't write in the book if you want to play with friends. **Answers on page 138.**

Scoring: Divide the number of seconds it took you to take the quiz by the number of questions you got correct. The lower your score, the better. For example, if it took you twenty seconds to get nine questions correctly answered, your score would be 2.2. If it took you twenty-five seconds to get all ten questions right, your score would be 2.5. So, in this case, speed was better than accuracy!

Hint: If you don't know an answer, skip it! Remember, the object of this quiz is not only to get as many correct answers as possible, but also to do it in as little time as possible.

1–3: Awesome!
4–6: Smarty-pants
7 & up: Not bad!

Fill in the blanks with either *Ocean*, *Sea*, *River*, or *Lake*:

1. Atlantic _____

2. _____ Superior

3. Dead _____

4. Adriatic _____

5. Indian _____

6. Mississippi _____

7. Yellow _____

8. _____ Titicaca

9. Arctic _____

10. Red _____

POSTCARDS FROM THE ROAD

There's no reason to wait until you get to your destination to write postcards to everyone you left behind. Send them postcards from wherever you are—car, plane, boat, or train! Draw the scene from your window, the rest stop or port you just left, or what the vehicle you're in looks like . . . whatever! When you're done, cut them out, stick them in an envelope, and send them on their way.

VANITY PLATE COLLECTION

Car owners who want to send a little message to the world—or at least to anyone they pass on the road—often pay a little extra to have a personalized message put on their license plates. On these pages, you can record the best vanity plates you come across in your travels.

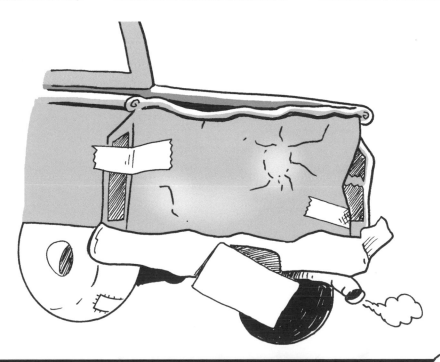

AREN'T THEY CUTE?!

The following couples just had babies. What do these little tikes look like?

Mr. Rooster and Mrs. Robot

Mr. Duck and Mrs. Lady Gaga

Mr. Elephant and Mrs. Volkswagen Beetle

Mr. Unicorn and Mrs. Rabbit

Mr. Elk and Mrs. Zebra

Mr. Penguin and Mrs. Worm

Mr. Peacock and Mrs. Watermelon

Mr. Koala and Mrs. Frog

Mr. Werewolf and Mrs. Grasshopper

Mr. Cat and Mrs. Dog

Mr. Panda and Mrs. Porcupine

Mr. Fox and Mrs. Eagle

Mr. Turtle and Mrs. Snail

Mr. Rhino and Mrs. Giraffe

Mr. C3P0 and Mrs. Barbie

Mr. Grizzly Bear and Mrs. Ant

Now come up with some of your own:

NAGS A RAM

If you move the letters in the title of this puzzle around, you get anagrams, which are words made from rearranging the letters of other words. For example, one possible anagram of my name, Joe Rhatigan, would be "I heart Joan G." (I have no idea who Joan G. is, but I guess I heart her!) Try creating anagrams for your name and the names of your friends. It's cool if you can create a phrase or short sentence that makes some sort of sense, but it's not necessary.

Name

_____

_____

_____

_____

_____

_____

_____

_____

_____

Anagram

_____

_____

_____

_____

_____

_____

_____

_____

_____

Use this space to figure out your anagrams.

Can you unscramble these anagrams? *Answers on page 138.*

Can you figure out who these anagrammed presidents are?

1. Be Ogre Hugs

2. Karma Cab Boa

3. Hairball Con Man

4. Reggae Toning Show

5. Horseman Jets Off

How about these entertainers and sports stars?

6. A Dry Tomb

7. Noble Jamers

8. Twisty Flora

9. Teachable Deep Sky

10. Use My Lyric

What about some favorite holidays?

11. A New Hello

12. Crash Mist

13. Date Any Snivel

14. Saving Knight

15. Cyanide Ended Pen

And finally, some RODs (Really Old Dudes):

16. Frank B Jamin' Linen

17. Willie Makes A Phrase

18. Sand Smoothie

19. Open Loan

20. Your Hind Hair

Hints

1. Son and father, same name; 2. Sasha and Malia are his kids; 3. Four score and seven years ago; 4. He was first; 5. He was third; 6. Patriotic quarterback; 7. Basketball champ; 8. Tall country singer; 9. Fergie belongs; 10. Used to be Hannah Montana; 11. Boo!; 12. Ho, ho, ho; 13. I ♠ you!; 14. Gobble gobble; 15. Colorful explosions; 16. Kite, string, key; 17. Bard; 18. Lightbulb guy; 19. Short general; 20. Magic man

FUTOSHIKI

The object of Futoshiki is to place the numbers 1 to 4 (or higher, depending on the size of the puzzle) so that each row and column contains each of the digits. Some of the numbers are provided for you already. Also, greater than and less than signs must be obeyed: The number on the open side of a < or > symbol must be larger than the number on the pointed side. **Answers on page 139.**

Sample Game

column column column column

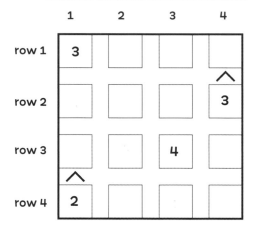

Step 1: It's always good to start by seeing if you can figure out any numbers based on the greater than and less than signs. In the first column, 2 is only greater than 1, so put the 1 in the box above the 2. This also lets you fill in the last blank box in that column: a 4.

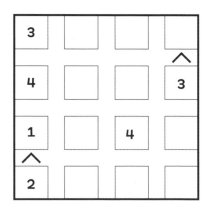

Step 2: The third row is missing a 3 and a 2. Since there's already a 3 in the second row, fourth column, the 3 in the third row has to go in the second column. This means the 2 goes in the last box in the third row. Now you can fill in the rest of the fourth column, since 3 is greater than 1.

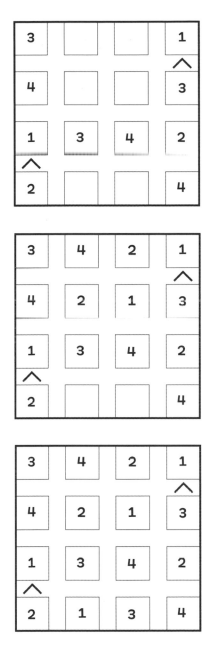

Step 3: The 4 in the first row can only go in the second square, since every other column already has a 4. Now you can fill in the box next to it with a 2. That 2 then shows that there's only one place left to place the 2 in the second row, and then the 1 in the same row.

Step 4: The last two empty squares are now easy to fill in. The second column needs a 1 and the third column needs a 3.

Tip: Often there will be two numbers or more that could fit in a certain box. Until you know for certain which number is the correct one, write both numbers in the box.

1.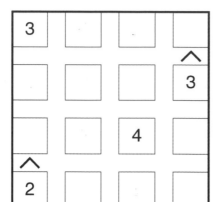

2.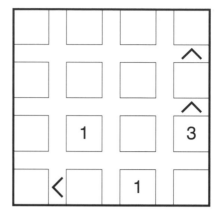

3.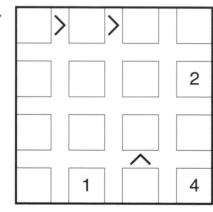

Now try a 5 x 5 puzzle, where you need to fill in the numbers 1 to 5.

4.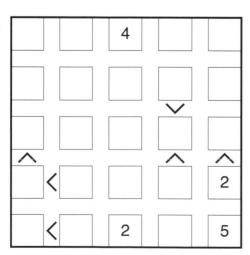

5.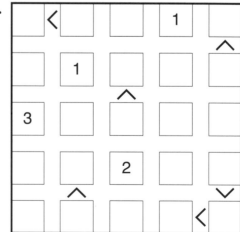

6.

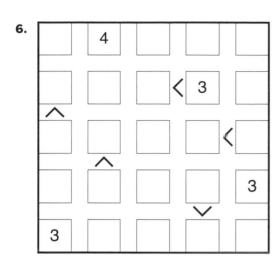

7.

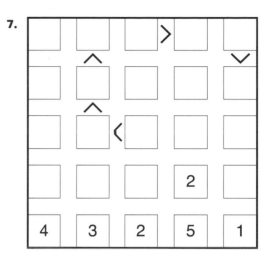

How about 6 x 6?

And finally, 7 x 7!

8.

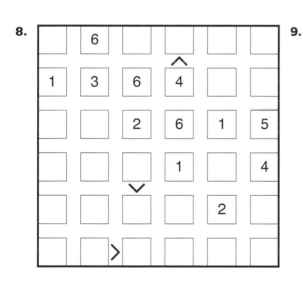

9.

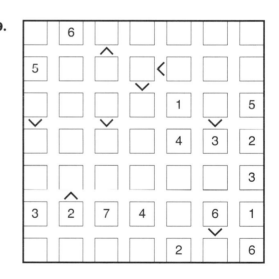

SPACE JAM

Imagine what a traffic jam in space would look like and doodle it here.

no
WARP
zone!

speed limit
186,000
miles per second!

UP AND DOWN THE MOUNTAIN

This is a simple game you can play by yourself or with travel mates. Using one of the game boards below and on the next page, climb and then descend the mountain by finding the numbers on license plates in numerical order. If you're playing with another person, the first one to go up and down the mountain wins. If you want to make it easier (for a younger sibling, for instance), you can cross off the numbers randomly as you find them.

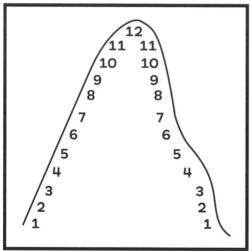
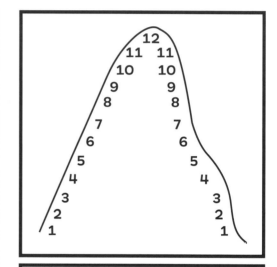
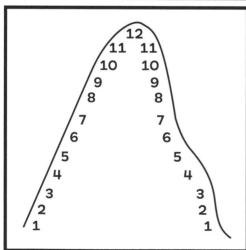
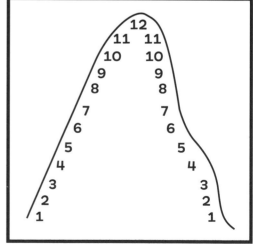

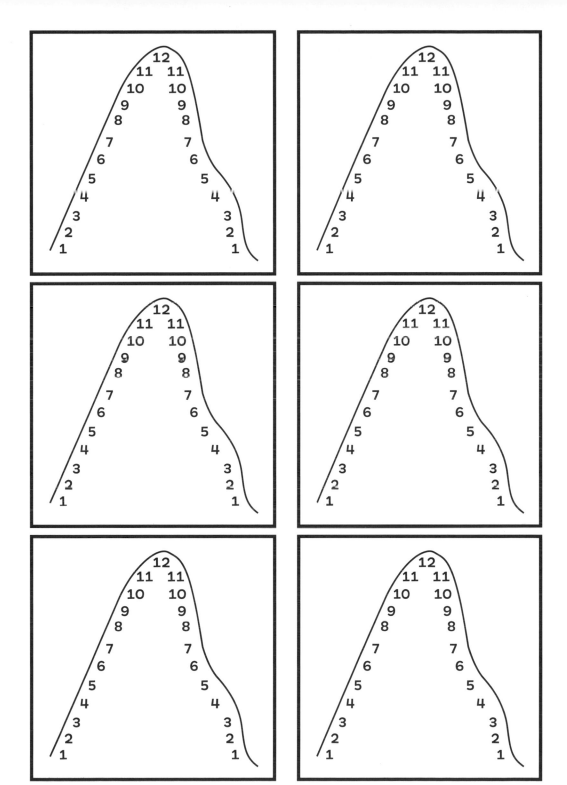

UP AND DOWN THE MOUNTAIN AGAIN

Same rules as the previous game, but this time you have to find these letter combinations in order!

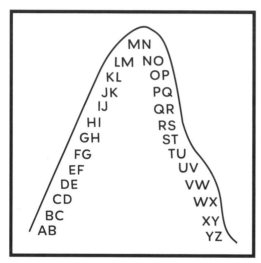

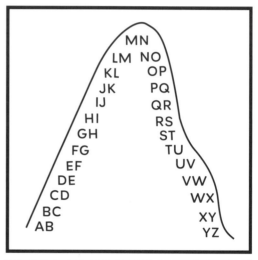

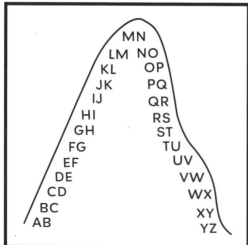

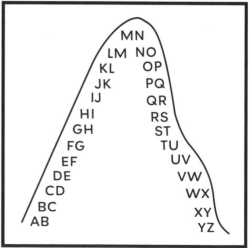

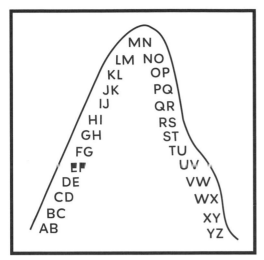
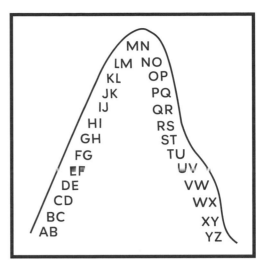
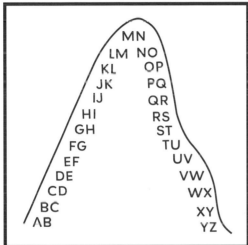
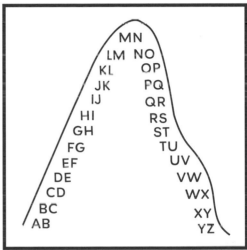
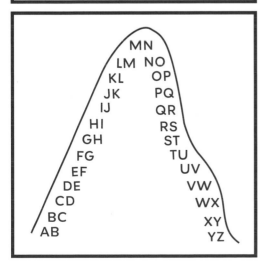
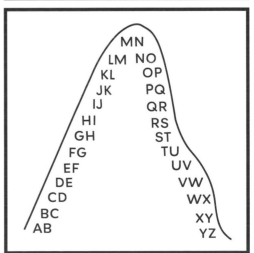

GUGGENHEIM

The object of this game is to name as many items in five categories as you can—and the more original you are, the more points you'll score!

What You Do

1. Each player uses one of the grids on the following pages.

2. Agree on five different categories, such as authors, countries, cartoon characters, song titles, cars, celebrities, etc. (Make sure to choose a category that has lots of potential answers. Cats, for instance, won't give you much to work with.)

3. Fill in the chosen categories along the top row of your grid—one category per column.

4. Agree on a five-letter word—or get someone else who isn't playing to choose one.

5. Place each letter of the word in a row along the left column of the grid.

Here's a sample grid:

	Authors	Songs	Relatives & Friends	Countries	Animals
P					
A					
R					
T					
Y					

6. Agree on an amount of time to play the game—say, five minutes. Use a timer or appoint a referee to say start and stop.

7. Once play begins, each player has to try to fill in all the boxes in the grid with words that fit in the category along the top row while also beginning with the letter in the first column. For instance, for the category *Authors* in the sample grid on the previous page, a player could write *J. K. Rowling* in the *R* row and *Aliki* in the *A* row. Fill in as many as you can come up with!

8. Once time is up, each player scores one point for every box filled in and two points for every word she comes up with that the other players don't have. The player with the highest point total wins.

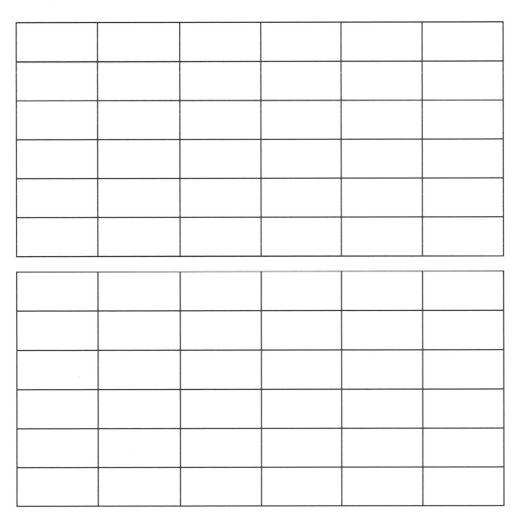

CARS, LOTS

Here is a giant list of cars that you might come across in your travels. Either by yourself or with whoever's in the backseat with you, cross off each car you find. You get extra points for listing cars you found that aren't on this list!

Acura
Alfa Romeo
Audi
BMW
Buick
Cadillac
Chevrolet
Chrysler
Citroën
Daihatsu
Daimler AG
Dodge
Ferrari
Fiat
Ford
GMC
Honda
Hummer
Hyundai
Infiniti
Isuzu
Jaguar
Jeep

Kia
Lamborghini
Land Rover
Lexus
Lincoln
Lotus
Maserati
Mazda
Mercedes-Benz
Mercury
MG
MINI
Mitsubishi
Nissan
Peugeot
Pontiac
Porsche
Renault
Rolls-Royce
Saab
Saturn
Scion
Subaru

Suzuki
Toyota
Volkswagen
Volvo

What else did you find?

_____
_____
_____
_____
_____
_____
_____
_____
_____
_____
_____

As of this writing, the list below consists of the top ten best-selling cars. Give yourself one hour or your whole trip and keep tabs on how many of each you see. Are they as popular where you're traveling as they are in the rest of the country? Use the rest of the space to draw their logos or the cars themselves.

Toyota Camry

_____

Honda Accord

_____

Chevrolet Silverado

_____

Ford F-Series (pickup truck)

_____

Toyota Prius

_____

Toyota Corolla

_____

Honda Civic

_____

Honda CR-V

_____

Chevrolet Malibu

_____

Ford Fusion

_____

IT'S YOUR JOB: CD COVER DESIGNER

The following bands need names for their new CDs as well as art for the covers. Don't let them down!

Sludge

Damaged Goodz

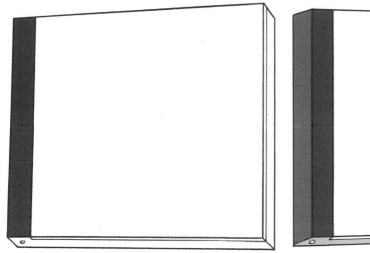

Battleaxe

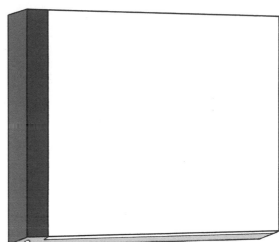

DJ Lipsink

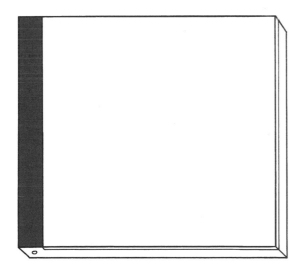

Li'l Whiner

Pirate Pete & the Treasure
Seekers

CROSS STREETS

Figure out the following street names with the clues provided so when someone asks directions, you know where to tell them to go. **Answers on page 139.**

For instance:

<u>Pork Product</u> Road and <u>Dairy Product</u> Avenue is:

Ham & Cheese

1. <u>Embraces</u> Avenue & <u>Smooches</u> Road

2. <u>Felines</u> Street & <u>Canines</u> Avenue

3. <u>Sleeping Place</u> Road & <u>Morning Meal</u> Street

4. <u>Dairy Product</u> Drive & <u>Hard Square Wheat Items</u> Avenue

5. <u>Woman Getting Married</u> Road & <u>Man Getting Married</u> Drive

6. <u>Heavenly Objects</u> Drive & <u>Zebra Pattern</u> Avenue

7. <u>Sodium Way</u> & <u>Ground Peppercorn</u> Avenue

8. <u>Fighting Road</u> & <u>Not Fighting</u> Way

9. <u>Winged Mammal Superhero</u> Avenue & <u>Sidekick Bird</u> Road

10. <u>Cleansing Agent</u> Way & <u>H^{2O}</u> Drive

Here are some blank street signs so you can make up your own funny cross streets!

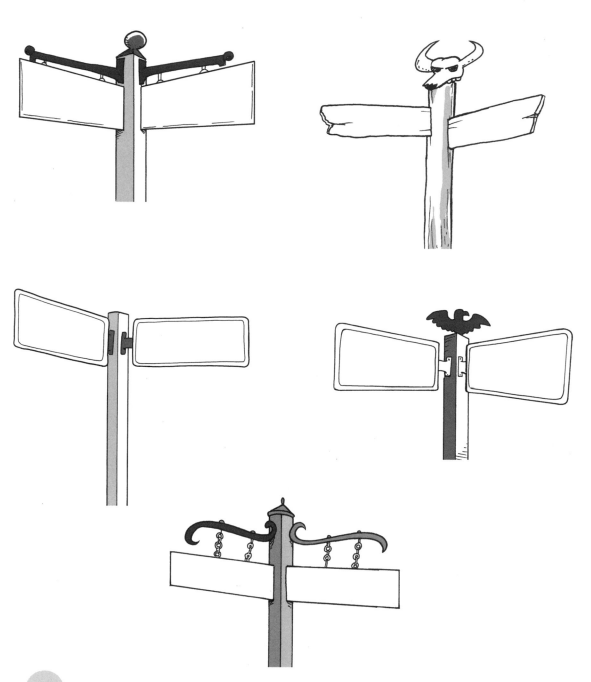

DON'T THINK TWICE: THE CLICHÉ EDITION

Answer the questions below as quickly as possible without putting too much thought into them. Time yourself and see how many you get right. Don't write in the book if you want to play with friends. **Answers on page 139.**

Scoring: Divide the number of seconds it took you to take the quiz by the number of questions you got correct. The lower your score, the better. For example, if it took you twenty seconds to get nine questions correctly answered, your score would be 2.2. If it took you twenty-five seconds to get all ten questions right, your score would be 2.5. So, in this case, speed was better than accuracy!

Hint: If you don't know an answer, skip it! Remember, the object of this quiz is not only to get as many correct answers as possible, but also to do it in as little time as possible.

1–3: Awesome!
4–6: Smarty-pants
7 & up: Not bad!

Fill in the blanks:

1. Signed, sealed, and _____.

2. Sticks and _____ will break my bones.

3. A _____ by any other name would smell as sweet.

4. An _____ a day keeps the doctor away.

5. The best thing since sliced _____.

6. He's got both _____ firmly planted on the ground.

7. Build a better _____ and the world will beat a path to your door.

8. Take the _____ by the horns.

9. That's the way the ball _____.

10. That's the way the cookie _____.

COLORFUL PHRASES

Match a color with the word or phrase to fill in the definitions. Colors can be used more than once and can be the first or last part of the word or phrase. Words and phrases are used only once. **Answers on page 140.**

1. _____: Doesn't happen often.
2. _____: Dollar bills
3. _____: An overnight plane flight
4. _____: The day after Thanksgiving, a big shopping day
5. _____: Scared
6. _____: Jealousy
7. _____: Healthy
8. _____: Cowardly
9. _____: A serious warning
10. _____: To speak a lot, rapidly
11. _____: Bruised
12. _____: Something not clearly defined
13. _____: Looking ill
14. _____: Something to distract from the real issue
15. _____: An event requiring one to wear formal clothing
16. _____: Very good
17. _____: Excessive complexity resulting in delay or inaction
18. _____: Every bad situation has some good in it
19. _____: Scandalous and/or false news reporting
20. _____: Born wealthy

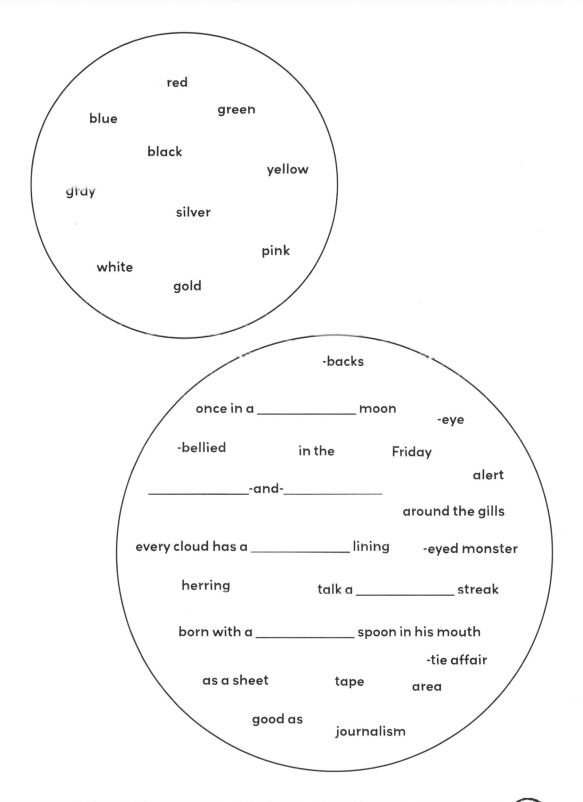

Circle 1 (colors):

red

blue green

black

yellow

gray

silver

pink

white

gold

Circle 2 (phrases):

-backs

once in a _____ moon

-eye

-bellied in the Friday

alert

_____-and-_____

around the gills

every cloud has a _____ lining -eyed monster

herring talk a _____ streak

born with a _____ spoon in his mouth

-tie affair

as a sheet tape area

good as

journalism

GRID ART

The images on this page and on page 74 have grids over them. Use the larger grids on the facing pages to enlarge these images. Simply draw what's in the grid boxes into the big grid boxes.

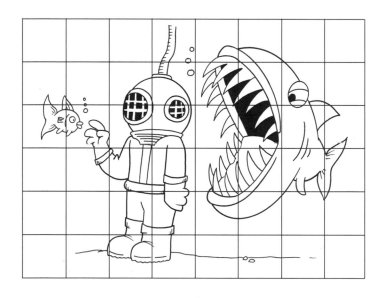

LICENSE PLATE MESSAGING

While navigating around the information superhighway, you may come across abbreviations and other shortcuts. Each license plate on the next two pages is one of these shortcuts. See if you can solve them all—or get a travel mate to help. **Answers on page 140.**

1
STATE
LOL

2
STATE
IMHO

3
STATE
BRB

4
STATE
ILBL8

5
STATE
B4N

6
STATE
BCNU

7
STATE
GR8

8
STATE
JK

9
STATE
TTYL

10 ROFL

11 TYVM

12 WYWH

13 TTFN

14 2G2BT

15 G2G

16 IDK

17 BTW

18 WTG

19 O RLY

20 IRL

21 1OQ

22 2BORNOT2B

23 14A&A41

24 ADIP

REST STOP

This game is just like the classic Battleship, except you're at a rest stop instead of the open seas and you're battling with parked cars instead of ships.

Object: Guess the location of all your opponent's vehicles at the rest stop.

What You Need

2 players

Pencil or pen for each player

What You Do

1. Tear out the grids on the following pages to play. Each player needs two grids: one to place his cars and trucks, and the other to note hits and misses. (When you run out of grids, create your own with graph paper.)
2. Without the other player seeing what you're doing, place your vehicles on one of the grids by shading in squares. These are the cars and trucks at your command:

   1 tractor trailer (5 squares)

   1 limousine (4 squares)

   1 SUV (3 squares)

   2 sedans (2 squares)

   2 hybrids (1 square)

For example:

3. Once each player has positioned his vehicles, take turns guessing where your opponent has hidden his vehicles by saying the letter and number of a particular square, such as E8.

4. The opponent says "miss" if you didn't hit a car (pick a square that is shaded in) and says "hit" if you did.

5. Mark the hit or miss on the second grid to keep track of your opponent's vehicles.

6. The first player to have all his vehicles hit loses.

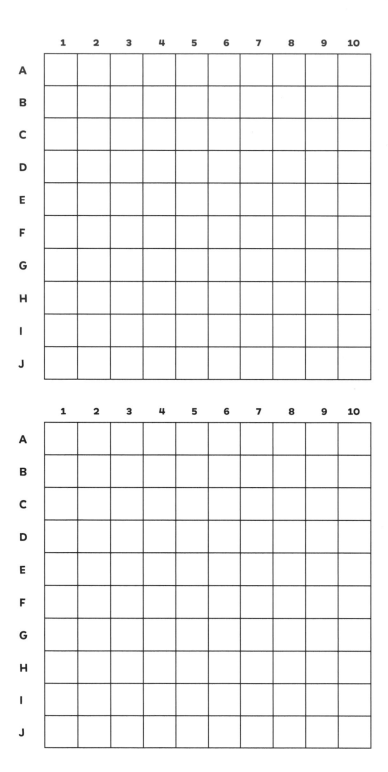

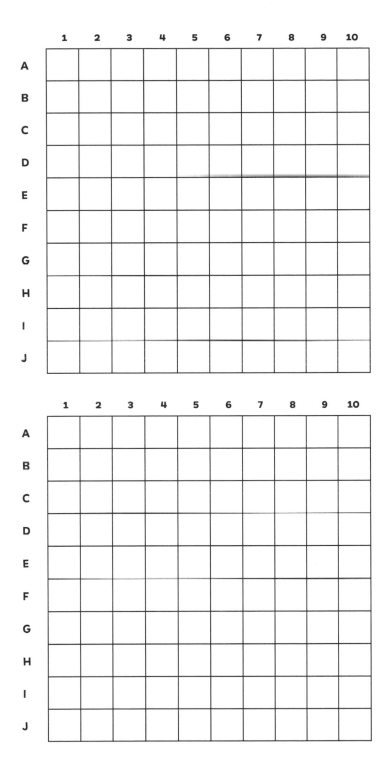

BUMPER STICKERS

Write in the best bumper stickers you come across in your travels.

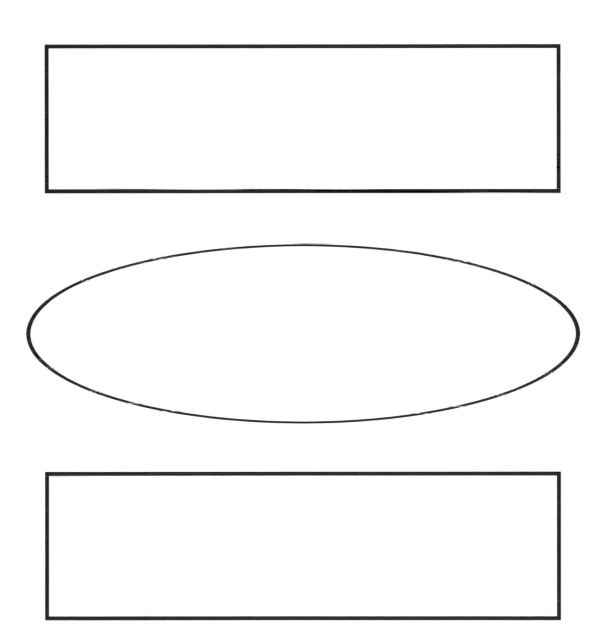

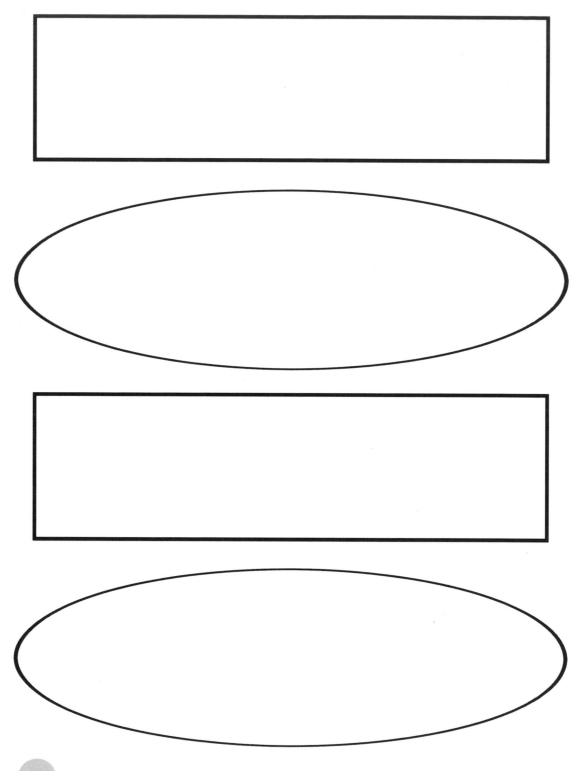

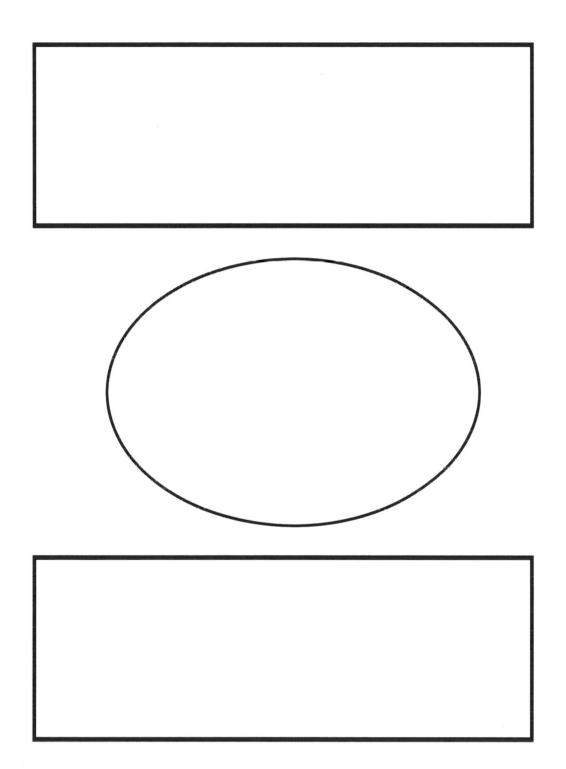

ROAD TRIP BINGO

This game is like a scavenger hunt, but it's also bingo. If you see it, cross it out. It could be something on the side of the road, in the next lane, or in the car ahead of you—but it can't be inside the car! The first person to cross out a diagonal, vertical, or horizontal line wins. Award a special prize to the first person to complete his or her board.

Squashed bug	Pothole	A farm	White pickup truck	Railroad Crossing sign
Pieces of a tire	Someone littering	Roadkill	Plastic bag litter	Convertible
Hybrid car	Really big flag	FREE	Tow truck	Dog with head out window
An RV	Road workers not working	A driver eating something	Water tower	Car missing license plate
Sports car speeding	Peeling billboard	"Welcome to _____" sign	Bike rack with at least three bikes	Misspelled sign

Squashed bug	Pothole	A farm	White pickup truck	Railroad Crossing sign
Pieces of a tire	Someone littering	Roadkill	Plastic bag litter	Convertible
Hybrid car	Really big flag	FREE	Tow truck	Dog with head out window
An RV	Road workers not working	A driver eating something	Water tower	Car missing license plate
Sports car speeding	Peeling billboard	"Welcome to _____" sign	Bike rack with at least three bikes	Misspelled sign

THE GREAT RADIO SCAVENGER HUNT

Play this game with the whole family the next time you're on a long car trip. Have the front-seat passenger turn the radio dial and the rest of you listen for the items below. Circle what you find.

1. Furniture commercial
2. Traffic update
3. Local weather forecast
4. Beatles song
5. Song to which at least one adult in the car knows all the words
6. Laughing
7. Crying
8. NPR station identification
9. Mention of a website
10. Love song
11. Contest announcement
12. Song with a saxophone
13. Song about driving
14. Sad country song
15. Opera song
16. Rap song
17. Two songs by the same artist
18. A contest in which you have to text the station
19. Weather alert test
20. Robot voice
21. A foreign language (to you)
22. Ad for used cars

23. Song with no words

24. Song older than the oldest person in the car

25. Ad for a lawyer

26. Clapping

27. Whistling

28. A banjo

29. Top music countdown

30. List of upcoming concerts nearby

31. Talk show

32. Silly sound effect

33. DJ making a mistake

34. Heavy metal song

35. Song with no drums

36. Patriotic song

37. Public service announcement

38. Phone ringing

39. DJ signing off for the day

40. Three songs in a row without interruption

41. Rolling Stones song

42. Rihanna song

43. Song with both singing and rapping

44. Person talking way too fast

45. DJ using the word *awesome* or *cool*

46. Michael Jackson song

47. Song that mentions a body part

48. Religious programming

49. Angry person talking about politics

50. An explosion sound

HE SAID WHAT?

Fill in the speech bubbles according to the directions.

What cows say when no one is looking.

What Venus de Milo says when her nose itches.

Junior ate something that didn't agree with him.

The presidents argue over who is touching whom.

Drivers remark on a surprising vehicle.

Mona Lisa and Vincent Van Gogh have a chat.

ROAD SIGNS

All these blank road signs need to be filled in.

LICENSE PLATE GAMES

It's always fun finding as many different license plates as possible on your trip. Use the map below to shade in the states, territories, and provinces you find.

The first person to find ten license plates with the letters or numbers in alphabetical or numerical order wins. For example, score a point for ACS but not for ASC.

Have half the car's inhabitants find the letters *A* through *Z* on license plates, in order. Meanwhile, have the other half look for letters *Z* through *A* on license plates, reversing the order. Who finds them all first?

Spend an hour finding as many words as possible on license plates. Vanity plates don't count! List them here:

_____

_____

_____

_____

_____

_____

Have someone choose a license plate with three or four letters on it. Everyone then has to come up with a short sentence where each word begins with the letters on the plate. For instance, if your chooser yells out, "DKR," you can say "Dull Kids Rule!" or "Don't Keep Radios." The car riders then vote on which was the best, weirdest, or most original sentence.

Pick a license plate at random and write down the letters on the plate. Then see who can spell the longest word using those letters in the same sequence they're in on the plate. For instance, say you find the letters *EAP*. You can create the words *hEAP* or *rEshAPe*.

Give each player twenty points. As you're driving along, place bets on what the first number (zero through nine) on the license plate of the next car that passes you will be. If you're right, you win the number of points you bet. If you're wrong, you lose those points.

As you pass cars, take turns adding up the numbers on their plates. (Ignore any letters on the plates.) When it's your turn again, add the total from the new plate to your previous total. When a player reaches one hundred points or more, finish the round so everyone's had an equal number of turns. Add up your scores. The highest score wins.

HOW MANY . . .

Count 'em up!
Answers on page 140.

. . . US presidents can you name?

_____
_____
_____
_____
_____
_____

. . . Summer Olympic sports can you name?

_____
_____
_____
_____

. . . Disney cartoon characters do you know?

_____
_____
_____
_____
_____
_____
_____

. . . of these acronyms (abbreviations using the first letter in each word) do you know?

1. ASPCA

_____

2. FBI

_____

3. CIA

_____

4. NATO

_____

5. FAQ

_____

6. NAACP

_____

7. NCAA

_____

8. ATM

_____

9. AOL

_____

10. CEO

_____

11. YMCA

_____

12. NFL

_____

13. ESPN

_____

14. NOW

_____

15. SWAT

_____

THE NAME GAME

Choose a first name from column 1 and a last name from column 2 to figure out who's who. For example: She loves layered Italian food. Name from column one: Liz. Name from column two: Onya. Name = Liz Onya . . . like lasagna—get it? **Answers on page 142.**

Column 1	Column 2
Anita	Key
Joe	Lynn
Rob	Baum
Ella	Burr
Rick	Bayer
Amanda	Bath
Lois	Lee
Ty	Price
Anna	Time
Chad	Dewitt
Hugh	Pipes
Justin	Thonn
Don	O'Shea
Teddy	Terbocks
Brock	Mull
Al	King
Duane	Mongous
Mary	D'Banque
Tim	Poe
Adam	Vader

1. His friends think he's cuddly and huggable.

_____

2. She smells bad and is dirty.

_____

3. He's not very good at spelling.

_____

4. He loves his vegetables.

_____

5. He's a comedian.

_____

6. She's beastly.

_____

7. He likes to volunteer.

_____

8. He steals for a living.

_____

9. He can't stop talking.

_____

10. She's moving up in the world.

_____

11. He's a plumber with a speech impediment.

_____

12. He's rather large.

_____

13. She runs long distances.

_____

14. He bounces around a lot.

_____

15. He's in the lumber industry.

_____

16. He's explosive.

_____

17. She has strings and plays music.

_____

18. He's stubborn and brays.

_____

19. He's never late for anything.

_____

20. She's always looking for a bargain.

_____

Bonus Round

Now try the same with the following first names, last names, and middle initials!

Column 1	Column 2	Column 3
Dan	U.	Gone
Curt	A.	Lyon
Will	B.	Ware
Al	B.	Mander
Jan	N.	Ball
Ann	D.	Byrd
Bea	E.	Dextrous
Earl	D.	Arry
Sal	E.	Rodd
Chuck	A.	Gator

21. He has many sharp teeth.

_____

22. He's leaving soon.

_____

23. He likes to hold up the drapes.

_____

24. He likes yellow flowers.

_____

25. She loves winter.

_____

26. She is very alert.

_____

27. She can throw with either hand.

_____

28. He's small and slithery.

_____

29. He likes to get up at dawn.

_____

30. He plays the outfield.

_____

DON'T THINK TWICE: THE PRONUNCIATION EDITION

Answer the questions below as quickly as possible without putting too much thought into them. Time yourself and see how many you get right. Don't write in the book if you want to play with friends.
Answers on page 142.

Scoring: Divide the number of seconds it took you to take the quiz by the number of questions you got correct. The lower your score, the better. For example, if it took you twenty seconds to get nine questions correctly answered, your score would be 2.2. If it took you twenty-five seconds to get all ten questions right, your score would be 2.5. So, in this case, speed was better than accuracy!

Hint: If you don't know an answer, skip it! Remember, the object of this quiz is not only to get as many correct answers as possible, but also to do it in as little time as possible.

1–3: Awesome!
4–6: Smarty-pants
7 & up: Not bad!

Match the word with its correct pronunciation:

1. capitulate
2. curious
3. confusion
4. cacophony
5. collaborate
6. chimera
7. charismatic
8. cartridge
9. custodian
10. cologne

a. *kär*-trij
b. kə-*la*-bə-rāt
c. kən-*fyü*-zhən
d. *kyur*-ē-əs
e. ker-əz-*ma*-tik
f. kə-*lōn*
g. kī-*mir*-ə
h. kə-*pi*-chə-lāt
i. ka-*kä*-fə-nē
j. kəs-*tō*-dē-ən

FAVORITE/LEST FAVORITE

	Favorite	Least Favorite
Song		
Band		
Breakfast food		
Lunch food		
Dinner food		
Drink		
Restaurant		
Ice cream flavor		
Candy bar		
Vegetable		
Fruit		
Color		
Season		
Holiday		
Month		
Day of the week		
Smell		
Memory		
Room in your house		
Sport		
Sports team		
Superhero		
School subject		
Book		
Movie		

	Favorite	Least Favorite
Television show		
Hobby		
Board game		
Computer game		
Website		
Wild animal		
Pet		
Celebrity		
Cartoon character		
World leader		
Country		
Chore		
Family ritual		

Write in your own topics:

	Favorite	Least Favorite

TRAVELING CIRCUS

It's time for the circus to pack up and move to the next city! Draw the circus performers and animals getting where they need to go.

COUNTDOWN

Who can find the longest word?

What You Do

1. Grab a travel mate and take turns choosing letters until you have nine. Write them down below.

2. Once you have your letters chosen, use the space below (or use separate pieces of paper) to come up with as many words as possible using only the nine letters you've chosen. You can only use each letter once.

3. The player with the longest word wins!

Place letters here:

_____ _____ _____ _____ _____ _____ _____ _____ _____

Your space: **Your friend's space:**

Place letters here:

_____ _____ _____ _____ _____ _____ _____ _____ _____

Your space: **Your friend's space:**

How many words can you create from the following words?

backgammon

_____

_____

_____

horseplay

_____

_____

_____

dominoes

_____

_____

_____

presidential

_____

_____

_____

entertainment

_____

_____

_____

dictionary

_____

_____

_____

antidisestablishmentarianism

_____

_____

_____

FAMOUS NUMBERS

Have everyone you're traveling with help out with this one. All the numbers below are famous—you all just need to figure out why. Write down what you come up with next to the number. For example, if the number is 4, you might write: Four is famous because July 4 is when we celebrate Independence Day! Feel free to argue about what makes each one the most famous.

13
_____

60
_____

2
_____

15
_____

32
_____

29
_____

24
_____

100
_____

47

7

12

26

9

3

52

18

5

1

4

SYNONYM CROSSWORDS

Find the words that mean the same thing as the title of each puzzle. Hints are given, but there are no up and down clues. Consulting a thesaurus is not considered cheating with these puzzles! **Answers on page 142.**

Crazy

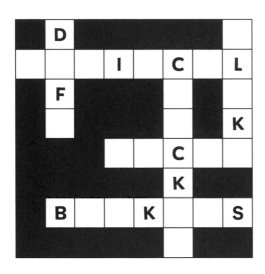

Big

Funny

Beautiful

Use these grids to make your own synonym puzzles for *smart,* *dangerous, sad,* **and** *happy.*

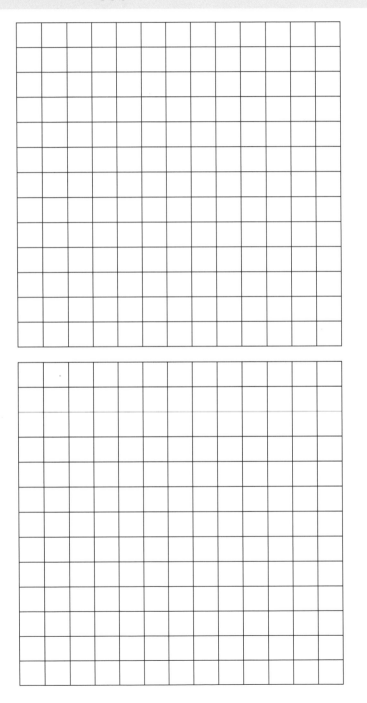

SILLY QUESTIONS

You provide the silly answers. *Some answers on page 143 ... but they're open to interpretation!*

1. What's the greatest use of cowhide?

_____

2. Why isn't your nose twelve inches long?

_____

3. If there are twenty blackbirds on a fence and you shoot one, how many are left?

_____

4. Some months have thirty days and some have thirty-one days. How many have twenty-eight days?

_____

5. What five-letter word can have its last four letters removed and still sound the same?

_____

6. A cowboy left on a trip on Friday, stayed for two days, and then returned on Friday. How is that possible?

_____

7. What has four wheels and flies?

_____

8. A man left home running. He ran a ways and then turned left, ran the same distance and turned left again, ran the same distance and turned left again. When he got home there were two masked men. Who were they?

_____

9. How far can you run into the woods?

_____

10. What makes a man bald?

_____

11. What always ends everything?

_____

12. A bird is sitting on a clothesline. How do you get your clothes off the line without bothering the bird?

_____

13. A person living in Georgia can't be buried in North Carolina. Why?

_____

14. What do caterpillars run away from?

_____

15. Why was the broom late for breakfast?

_____

16. What did one eye say to the other?

_____

17. What starts with _P_, ends with _E_, and has thousands of letters in it?

_____

18. What has no beginning, no middle, and no end?

_____

19. What word do you get if you turn the word _good_ upside down?

_____

20. What can you not keep until you have given it?

_____

IN BETWEEN

The object of this game is to find words that begin with the letters in the word on the left-hand column and end with the letters in the word on the right-hand column.

Example:

B	business	S
I	ice	E
R	ride	E
D	diamond	D

Scoring: 3 points for a common word, 2 points for a place name, and 1 point for a person's first or last name.

1.

C		D
A		O
T		G

Top score: 9
Your score:

2.

S		S
W		A
E		L
E		T
T		Y

Top score: 15
Your score:

3.

W   M
A   A
T   K
C   E
H   R

Top score: 15
Your score.

4.

H   T
O   O
M   W
E   N

Top score: 12
Your score:

5.

D   D
A   R
N   E
C   A
E   M

Top score: 15
Your score:

6.

E   S
L   T
E   R
P   O
H   L
A   L
N   E
T   R

Top score: 24
Your score:

7.

I	T
N	O
B	D
O	A
X	Y

Top score: 15
Your score:

8.

S	K
P	N
O	I
O	F
N	E

Top score: 15
Your score:

9.

H	F
A	O
N	O
D	T

Top score: 12
Your score:

10.

P	P
O	R
L	E
I	S
T	I
I	D
C	E
I	N
A	T
N	S

Top score: 30
Your score:

URIED CITIΞS

Take turns burying cities and finding them.

What You Do

1. A city is "buried" when its letters are placed in the right order in a sentence, but so distributed that the word is not easily found. For example, can you find the city in this sentence?

Put your shawl on; do not pin it.

It may take a moment, but sooner or later you will find *l on do n* (London).

2. Take turns with whoever wants to play. Each player comes up with a sentence with a buried city for the others to find.

3. Whoever finds the most cities wins.

Sentence: _____

Solution: _____

Sentence: _____

Solution: _____

Sentence: _____

Solution: _____

Sentence: _____

Solution: _____

Sentence: _____

Solution: _____

Sentence: _____

Solution: _____

Sentence: _____

Solution: _____

ABBREVIATED LYRICS

The following are the first letters of the words of well-known songs. For example, can you guess what song begins this way?

M H A L L, L L, L L. M H A L L W F W W A S

What if we told you it's about a girl and her fluffy pet? Hopefully you got that this is "Mary had a little lamb, little lamb, little lamb. Mary had a little lamb whose fleece was white as snow."

See if you can figure out what songs these abbreviated lyrics come from. Hints appear upside down on the next page. **Answers on page 143.**

1. O, S C Y S, B T D E L

2. T, T, L S, H I W W Y A

3. T W A F H A D, A B W H N-o

4. Y D W T T R O A P, S A F I H C A C I M

5. F J, F J, D V? D V? S L M, S L M, D D D, D D D

6. D T T S I A O H O S, O T F W G, L A T W

7. I A L T, S A S, H I M H, H I M S

8. O, S, D Y C F M. I C F A W M B O M K

9. O M H A F, E, I, E, I, O

10. S, S, S T M L. S, S, S T M L. S, S, S T M L. S T M L, M D

11. T M O T T B G. T M O W T C. B M S P A C J. I D C I I N G B

12. T W O T B G R A R, R A R, R A R. T W O T B G R A R, A T T T

13. Y A M S, M O S. Y M M H W S A G. Y N K, D, H M I L Y. P D T M S A

14. T B M, T B M, S H T R, S H T R. T A R A T F W. S C O T T W A C K

15. T O M, H P O. H P K-K O M T, W A K-K P-W, G A D A B, T O M C R H

Use this space to come up with your own abbreviated lyrics. Try them out on your travel mates!

_____

_____

_____

_____

_____

_____

_____

_____

Hints
1. Face the flag when you sing this.
2. Are those diamonds up there?
3. His name is also a game.
4. That's a funny name for a cap.
5. The French singing about Brother John.
6. Only sung in December. Lots of laughing and horse riding.
7. A little beverage holder shouts!
8. It must be hard to walk with that on your knee.
9. Read the last five letters out loud.
10. There's a whole lot of skipping going on.
11. Three strikes and you're out!
12. Baby's favorite bus song.
13. You brighten up the singer's day—in fact, you give her sunburn.
14. Non-seeing rodents dash.
15. Knicks, whacks, old men, and dog treats.

MINI CROSSWORDS

These bite-size nugget crosswords are great for when you only have a few minutes (or if you have little patience!). The only thing is, you have to figure out which boxes the answers of the clues belong to.
Answers on page 144.

ANIMAL SOUNDS

Clues
Woof
Meow
Baaa (but not the first *Baaa* you think of)
Beast of burden whose sound is not commonly known—it sort of lows and moos and whatnot

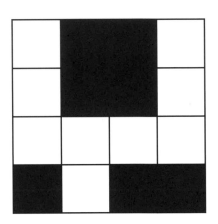

COMMON SENSES

Clues
All the better to hear you with
All the better to smell you with
All the better to see you with
All the better to touch you with
All the better to taste you with

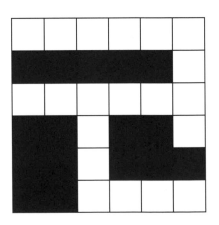

GETTING AROUND

Clue
Four modes of transportation

INTERIOR BODY PARTS

Clues
Detoxes the body and helps in
 digestion, among other things
Where the food goes
You need these to breathe
Bodybuilders flex them
They're strong, but can break when
 you fall

WHEN WE MEET & DEPART

Clues
A simple, friendly greeting
An even simpler friendly greeting
Spanish so long
So long
Cowboy greeting
Spanish greeting

HERE THERE BE MONSTERS

Long ago, people believed the open sea was full of monsters. What creatures can you imagine living underwater? Use the squiggles to start your own watery beasts, and then create more of your own!

C4N YOU R3AD 7H15?
P4R7 7WO

The Internet is full of silly things to do and read. Here's something that's been kicking around there awhile. Can you read it?

7H15 M3554G3
53RV35 7O PR0V3
H0W 0UR M1ND5 C4N
D0 4M4Z1NG 7H1NG5!
1MPR3551V3 7H1NG5!
1N 7H3 B3G1NN1NG
17 WA5 H4RD, BU7
N0W, 0N 7H15 L1N3,
Y0UR M1ND 1S
R34D1NG 17
4U70M471C4LLY
W17H0U7 3V3N
7H1NK1NG 4B0U7 17.
B3 PROUD! 0NLY
C3R741N P30PL3 C4N
R3AD 7H15.
PL3453 F0RW4RD 1F
Y0U C4N R34D 7H15.

Turn to page 144 if you are having trouble making out some of the words. Now, create your own messages and see if anyone else can read them.

Write your message with normal letters here:

_____

_____

_____

_____

_____

_____

_____

Now, make the following substitutions:

0 for O
4 for A
3 for E
1 for I
5 for S
7 for T

Rewrite your message with the substitutions here:

_____

_____

_____

_____

_____

_____

_____

CREATE YOUR OWN RESTAURANT

On your travels you may end up stopping at a lot of restaurants—and if you're a picky eater, they may never have just what you're looking for. Use this space to come up with your own restaurant.

First, create the perfect menu:

What's the name of your restaurant?

_____

Design your restaurant's logo here:

Now place your logo and restaurant name on these items and place your food of choice in the containers.

WHAT WOULD . . .

Draw 'em as you see 'em!

. . . a monkey movie star look like?

. . . an elephant who robbed convenience stores look like?

. . . a vampire kitten look like?

...a Frankenstein's monster dog look like?

...a hairy pair of binoculars look like?

...a man with eyes on his hands look like?

. . . a woman with ears on her knees look like?

. . . a Styrofoam house look like?

. . . a painting look like if the artist had to use her hair as a paintbrush?

. . . a painting look like if the artist had to use his feet as a paintbrush?

. . . a bank look like if we used teddy bears as money?

. . . our wallets look like if we used teddy bears as money?

THE WHERE I WENT SUPER QUIZ

After you come home from your fabulous adventure, come up with fifteen facts about the trip. Then create a multiple choice quiz for those who went on the trip with you or for the folks who didn't get to go. It's a fun way to "tell" them about your trip!

1. _____
   a.
   b.
   c.
   d.

2. _____
   a.
   b.
   c.
   d.

3. _____
   a.
   b.
   c.
   d.

4. _____
   a.
   b.
   c.
   d.

5. _____
   a.
   b.
   c.
   d.

6. _____
   a.
   b.
   c.
   d.

7. _____
   a.
   b.
   c.
   d.

8. _____
   a.
   b.
   c.
   d.

9. _____
   a.
   b.
   c.
   d.

10. _____
   a.
   b.
   c.
   d.

11. _____
   a.
   b.
   c.
   d.

12. _____
   a.
   b.
   c.
   d.

13. _____

    a.

    b.

    c.

    d.

14. _____

    a.

    b.

    c.

    d.

15. _____

    a.

    b.

    c.

    d.

Write your answers here, upside down:

13. _____ 14. _____ 15. _____
10. _____ 11. _____ 12. _____
7. _____ 8. _____ 9. _____
4. _____ 5. _____ 6. _____
1. _____ 2. _____ 3. _____

ANSWERS

THE ANSWERS

Wacky Words of Weirdness (page 4)

1. commonplace; 2. loner; 3. easy; 4. research; 5. tenor; 6. doozy;
7. stuffy; 8. realize; 9. tire; 10. detest

Word Jumbles (page 12)

1. city, function, rebel, grape: BUCCANEER; 2. Napoleon, Beyonce,
Cher, Prince, Sting: ROBERTO; 3. today, bisect, expand, digest: BYE,
SON; 4. erode, click, naptime, sister: MICE KRISPIES; 5. macaroni,
muscle, regret, bravery: GUMMY BEAR

Can You Raed Tihs? (page 14)

1. Mary had a little lamb
   Whose fleece was white as snow;
   And everywhere that Mary went,
   The lamb was sure to go.

2. Old King Cole was a merry old soul
   And a merry old soul was he;
   He called for his pipe and he called for his bowl
   And he called for his fiddlers three.

3. Little boy blue, come blow your horn.
   The sheep's in the meadow, the cow's in the corn.
   But where's the boy who looks after the sheep?
   He's under a haystack, fast asleep.

4. Everything happens for a reason; 5. Always a bridesmaid, never the
   bride; 6. His bark is worse than his bite; 7. A penny saved is a penny
   earned; 8. Don't throw the baby out with the bathwater; 9. Slow
   and steady wins the race; 10. Well done is better than well said;
   11. Attitude is a little thing that makes a big difference; 12. Thinking
   is the hardest work there is, which is probably why so few engage

in it; 13. Minds are like parachutes: They only function when they are open; 14. Everything should be made as simple as possible . . . but not simpler; 15. Twenty years from now you will be more disappointed by the things you didn't do than by the ones you did.

Off with Its Head! (page 24)
1. crib = rib; 2. beast = east; 3. ranger = anger; 4. crash = rash; 5. rash = ash; 6. touch = ouch; 7. pirate = irate; 8. story = Tory; 9. flab = lab; 10. flint = lint; 11. brain = rain; 12. sham = ham; 13. coral = oral; 14. spout = pout; 15. pout = out; 16. speech = peach; 17. verb = herb; 18. whale = hail; 19. third = herd; 20. bacon = achin'

Place Names (page 30)
1. Italy; 2. Australia; 3. California; 4. India; 5. Greenland; 6. Alaska; 7. South America; 8. China; 9. Florida; 10. Mexico; 11. Africa; 12. Maine; 13. United Kingdom; 14. New York; 15. Europe

Don't Think Twice: The Bodies of Water Edition (page 32)
1. Ocean; 2. Lake; 3. Sea (even though it's a lake, it's called the Dead Sea!); 4. Sea; 5. Ocean; 6. River; 7. River; 8. Lake; 9. Ocean; 10. Sea

Nags a Ram (page 46)
1. George Bush; 2. Barack Obama; 3. Abraham Lincoln; 4. George Washington; 5. Thomas Jefferson; 6. Tom Brady; 7. LeBron James; 8. Taylor Swift; 9. The Black Eyed Peas; 10. Miley Cyrus; 11. Halloween; 12. Christmas; 13. Valentine's Day; 14. Thanksgiving; 15. Independence Day; 16. Benjamin Franklin; 17. William Shakespeare; 18. Thomas Edison; 19. Napoleon; 20. Harry Houdini

Futoshiki (page 48)

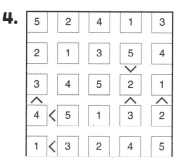

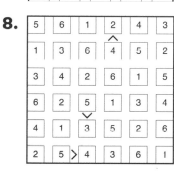

1.
3	4	2	1
4	2	1	3
1	3	4	2
2	1	3	4

2.
3	2	4	1
1	4	3	2
4	1	2	3
2	3	1	4

3.
4	2	1	3
1	3	4	2
3	4	2	1
2	1	3	4

4.
5	2	4	1	3
2	1	3	5	4
3	4	5	2	1
4	5	1	3	2
1	3	2	4	5

5.
4	5	3	1	2
2	1	4	3	5
3	2	5	4	1
1	3	4	2	5
5	4	1	2	3

6.
2	4	3	5	1
4	2	1	3	5
5	3	4	1	2
1	5	2	4	3
3	1	5	2	4

7.
2	1	4	3	5
5	2	1	4	3
3	4	5	1	2
1	5	3	2	4
4	3	2	5	1

8.
5	6	1	2	4	3
1	3	6	4	5	2
3	4	2	6	1	5
6	2	5	1	3	4
4	1	3	5	2	6
2	5	4	3	6	1

9.
2	6	1	7	3	5	4
5	4	2	3	6	1	7
4	3	6	2	1	7	5
1	7	5	6	4	3	2
6	1	4	5	7	2	3
3	2	7	4	5	6	1
7	5	3	1	2	4	6

Cross Streets (page 66)

1. Hugs & Kisses; 2. Cats & Dogs; 3. Bed & Breakfast; 4. Cheese & Crackers; 5. Bride & Groom; 6. Stars & Stripes; 7. Salt & Pepper; 8. War & Peace; 9. Batman & Robin; 10. Soap & Water

Don't Think Twice: The Cliché Edition (page 69)

1. delivered; 2. stones; 3. rose; 4. apple; 5. bread; 6. feet; 7. mousetrap; 8. bull; 9. bounces; 10. crumbles

Colorful Phrases (page 70)

1. once in a blue moon; 2. greenbacks; 3. red-eye; 4. Black Friday; 5. White as a sheet. 6. green-eyed monster; 7. in the pink; 8. yellow-bellied; 9. red alert; 10. talk a blue streak; 11. black-and-blue; 12. gray area; 13. green around the gills; 14. red herring; 15. white-tie or black-tie affair; 16. good as gold; 17. red tape; 18. every cloud has a silver lining; 19. yellow journalism; 20. born with a silver spoon in his mouth

License Plate Messaging (page 76)

1. laughing out loud; 2. in my humble opinion; 3. be right back; 4. I'll be late; 5. bye for now; 6. be seeing you; 7. great; 8. just kidding; 9. talk to you later; 10. rolling on floor laughing; 11. thank you very much; 12. wish you were here;. 13. ta-ta for now; 14. too good to be true; 15. got to go; 16. I don't know; 17. by the way; 18. way to go; 19. oh, really; 20. in real life; 21. thank you; 22. to be or not to be; 23. all for one and one for all; 24. another day in paradise

How Many . . . (page 96)

Presidents:

1	1789–1797	George Washington
2	1797–1801	John Adams
3	1801–1809	Thomas Jefferson
4	1809–1817	James Madison
5	1817–1825	James Monroe
6	1825–1829	John Quincy Adams
7	1829–1837	Andrew Jackson
8	1837–1841	Martin Van Buren
9	1841	William Henry Harrison
10	1841–1845	John Tyler
11	1845–1849	James K. Polk
12	1849–1850	Zachary Taylor
13	1850–1853	Millard Fillmore
14	1853–1857	Franklin Pierce
15	1857–1861	James Buchanan
16	1861–1865	Abraham Lincoln
17	1865–1869	Andrew Johnson
18	1869–1877	Ulysses S. Grant

19	1877–1881	Rutherford B. Hayes
20	1881	James Garfield
21	1881–1885	Chester Arthur
22	1885–1889	Grover Cleveland
23	1889–1893	Benjamin Harrison
24	1893–1897	Grover Cleveland
25	1897–1901	William McKinley
26	1901–1909	Theodore Roosevelt
27	1909–1913	William Taft
28	1913–1921	Woodrow Wilson
29	1921–1923	Warren G. Harding
30	1923–1929	Calvin Coolidge
31	1929–1933	Herbert Hoover
32	1933–1945	Franklin Delano Roosevelt
33	1945–1953	Harry S. Truman
34	1953–1961	Dwight D. Eisenhower
35	1961–1963	John F. Kennedy
36	1963–1969	Lyndon B. Johnson
37	1969–1974	Richard M. Nixon
38	1974–1977	Gerald R. Ford
39	1977–1981	Jimmy E. Carter, Jr.
40	1981–1989	Ronald W. Reagan
41	1989–1993	George H. W. Bush
42	1993–2001	William Jefferson Clinton
43	2001–2009	George W. Bush
44	2009–	Barack H. Obama

Summer Olympic Sports:
archery, badminton, basketball, boxing, canoeing & kayaking, cycling, diving, equestrian, fencing, field hockey, gymnastics, handball, judo, modern pentathlon, rowing, rugby, sailing, shooting, soccer, swimming, table tennis, tae kwon do, tennis, track & field, triathlon, volleyball, weight lifting, wrestling

Acronyms:
1. the American Society for the Prevention of Cruelty to Animals;
2. the Federal Bureau of Investigation; 3. the Central Intelligence

Agency; 4. the North Atlantic Treaty Organization; 5. Frequently Asked Questions; 6. the National Association for the Advancement of Colored People; 7. the National Collegiate Athletic Association; 8. Automated Teller Machine; 9. America Online; 10. Chief Executive Officer; 11. Young Men's Christian Association; 12. National Football League; 13. Entertainment and Sports Programming Network; 14. the National Organization for Women; 15. Special Weapons and Tactics

The Name Game (page 98)

1. Teddy Bayer; 2. Anita Bath; 3. Ty Poe; 4. Brock Lee; 5. Joe King; 6. Anna Mull; 7. Al Dewitt; 8. Rob D'Banque; 9. Chad Terbocks; 10. Ella Vader; 11. Duane Pipes; 12. Hugh Mongous; 13. Mary Thonn; 14. Rick O'Shea; 15. Tim Burr; 16. Adam Baum; 17. Amanda Lynn; 18. Don Key; 19. Justin Time; 20. Lois Price; 21. Al E. Gator; 22. Will B. Gone; 23. Curt N. Rodd; 24. Dan D. Lyon; 25. Jan U. Arry; 26. Bea A. Ware; 27. Ann B. Dextrous; 28. Sal A. Mander; 29. Earl. E. Byrd; 30. Chuck D. Ball

Don't Think Twice: The Pronunciation Edition (page 101)

1. h; 2. d; 3. c; 4. i; 5. b; 6. g; 7. e; 8. a; 9. j; 10. f

Synonym Crosswords (page 110)

Crazy

Big

Funny

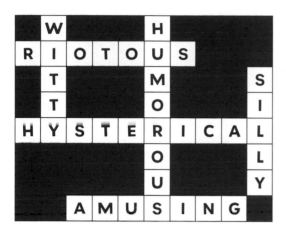

Beautiful

Silly Questions (page 114)

1. To cover cows; 2. Because then it would be a foot; 3. None: They would all fly away at the sound of the gun; 4. They *all* have at least twenty-eight days; 5. Queue; 6. His horse's name is Friday; 7. A garbage truck; 8. A catcher and an umpire; 9. Halfway, because after that, you're running *out of* the woods; 10. A lack of hair; 11. The letter *g*; 12. Wait until the bird flies away; 13. The person is still *living*; 14. Dogerpillars; 15. He swept in; 16. Between you and me, something smells; 17. Post office; 18. A doughnut; 19. It's still *good*, it's just upside down now; 20. A promise

Abbreviated Lyrics (page 120)

1. "The Star Spangled Banner"; 2. "Twinkle, Twinkle, Little Star"; 3. "Bingo"; 4. "Yankee Doodle"; 5. "Frère Jacques"; 6. "Jingle Bells"; 7. "I'm a Little Teapot"; 8. "Oh, Susanna"; 9. "Old MacDonald"; 10. "Skip to My Lou"; 11. "Take Me Out to the Ball Game"; 12. "The Wheels on the Bus"; 13. "You Are My Sunshine"; 14. "Three Blind Mice"; 15. "This Old Man"

Mini Crosswords (page 122)

Animal Sounds

Common Senses

Getting Around

Interior Body Parts

When We Meet & Depart

C4N Y0U R3AD 7H15? P4R7 7W0 (page 126)

This message serves to prove how our minds can do amazing things! Impressive things! In the beginning it was hard, but now, on this line, your mind is reading it automatically without even thinking about it. Be proud! Only certain people can read this. Please forward if you can read this.